PIECE
BY
PIECE
THE
HEART
UNDERSTANDS

ROSARIO OZUNA

# PIECE BY PIECE THE HEART UNDERSTANDS

*Piece by Piece the Heart Understands*
ISBN: 979-8-218-44398-6 (Hardcover)
Library of Congress Control Number: 2024911932
Poetry - American. Poetry - World. Poetry - Young Adult.
Fiction – Short Stories. Poetry - Collection.

Copyright © 2024
Authored by: Rosario Ozuna
Cover Design by:
Mia Anahí Martínez
Edited by: Aldo González
Printed in the United States of America

# REVIEWS

"*Piece by Piece the Heart Understands* by Rosario Ozuna captivated me from the beginning to the end. Her story canvases about the dynamics of relationships, self-love, and finding yourself challenged me to complete my personal self-inventory, and it will challenge you. I love how she threads realistic scenarios in her works, which will allow the reader to know that he or she isn't alone in dealing with various issues. Her beautiful artwork continues to blow me away and each piece compliments her works, perfectly. If you haven't read anything by Mrs. Ozuna, then her second book is a great place to start. Mrs. Ozuna's book will trigger internal emotions and leave you contemplating about her stories… long after you complete. I look forward to her next book!"

~ Miracle Austin, author of *Doll* Trilogy, *Boundless*, and *FRIGHT BITES*

"Often, it feels as though life's events unfold beyond our control, leaving us with a sense of being misunderstood. Rosario Ozuna's poems delve into everyday situations and profound life events, offering diverse perspectives that emphasize resilience and personal growth. I found the book particularly impactful in how it validates adolescents, giving them a sense of recognition and self-worth. It speaks to both teenagers and adults who have encountered comparable challenges, resonating deeply with their experiences. I highly recommend including *Piece by Piece the Heart Understands* in your personal library collection."

~ Nancy Yvette Peña, Middle School Counselor

# DEDICATION

To the hearts and minds who may be grappling with the complexities of relationships and the ups and downs of everyday life, I offer this book as a beacon of hope and support. You are not alone in your journey, and I want you to know that there are people who understand, care, and want to guide you through the challenges you may face.

It's important to remember that a controlling partner may demand all of your attention, and it's easy to assume that this is a sign of love. However, it's crucial to recognize that this is not a healthy or balanced relationship. Instead, you deserve to prioritize your own needs and well-being, and seek help if you're in a situation where your safety is at risk.

The good news is that there are resources available to support you in learning how to manage these experiences and develop healthy boundaries. You don't have to face these challenges alone.

At the same time, I want to remind you that not every relationship or experience is negative. There are many wonderful things in life, and it's essential to appreciate and cherish these moments. Remember, asking for help is a sign of strength, not weakness. Please don't hesitate to reach out for support when you need it.

Through these poems, you will gain a deeper understanding of the importance of embracing one's true self, treating oneself and others with kindness, and cultivating supportive relationships that foster personal growth and success. The book serves as a powerful reminder that it's okay to be vulnerable and authentic, and that by doing so, we can build stronger connections with others and navigate life's challenges with greater ease. The poems acknowledge that it's okay to acknowledge our mistakes and to process our emotions, but the key is to find a way to rise above, move forward, and do not cease to believe in yourself.

# TABLE OF CONTENTS

"Remember, everyone's a READER; some of you haven't found the RIGHT book!"

What if, *Piece by Piece the Heart Understands* is that right book for you?

Don't stop reading until you find that right book!

~ *Rosario Ozuna*

# INTRODUCTION

Have you ever felt like you've found your perfect soulmate? You feel like you finally met your better half. How did you meet? Did he/she bump into you? Did you bump into him/her? Did your eyes meet as you both were passing each other? Everyone has a love story. But, I dare to ask: Is it a healthy one? Did he or she break the circle of trust somehow? Perhaps, it is a beautiful and healthy relationship. You're both young and full of life.

Then there's that first fight and he or she reveals his or her true colors. But since you're deeply in love with your partner or you've invested so much time into each other, you refuse to see that the slap, the pinch or bruise on your arm he or she just gave you is the first red flag that this is not a safe relationship. Perhaps he or she did not do any of those things, but screamed at you in a way he/she had never done so. Perhaps he or she pushed you, but not enough to hurt you. Regardless, these are not healthy behaviors in a partner and you need to be careful. These are signs that tell you it's the beginning of an endless trip of suffering and pain although you may not see it as such, because somehow you are in denial. And deep down you want to believe it is nothing simply because of an apology or a promise that it will not happen again, so you both continue together. Until?

Perhaps you are not going through this, perhaps it is your friend or a cousin, or someone you don't know. But if you read this book's poems, I hope they help you recognize the signs of an unhealthy relationship and avoid one. Although these things do happen, there are many healthy relationships out there. There are happy couples and many go through several ups and downs and make it work. But these couples do not harm each other the way these characters harm their loved one. Just remember, there are people that care and will help you if you ever find yourself in a toxic relationship. Please reach out to someone before it is too late.

In addition, these poems discuss themes about good or bad friendships, the beauty of love, and the sense of believing in oneself and moving forward after encountering a negative situation. Furthermore, they emphasize suggestions on how we ought to manage these circumstances. How should you react to these situations? Should you show others how you feel? Should you allow them to know that you've ignored the situation as if it does not bother you? It is okay to acknowledge that we've made a wrong decision or to break down and cry. But the most important thing is to find a way to stand up again and keep moving!

This book will help you connect with these situations or make you aware that these experiences do occur. Overall, the message is about embracing one's authentic self, being kind to oneself and others, and cultivating positive relationships that support personal growth and success.

These themes are interconnected. When we love ourselves, we're more likely to believe in our abilities and respect our own needs. When we believe in ourselves, we're more likely to love ourselves and know that we are our own number one. By embracing these themes, we can cultivate a deeper sense of self-love, self-acceptance, and personal growth.

Remember, piece by piece your heart will understand your situation and help you move forward.

Key takeaways include:

* Believe in yourself and never give up on your goals
* Respect yourself and others
* Think before you act and follow your inner guidance (GLOW)
* Surround yourself with good friends who value and support you
* Avoid toxic relationships and people who don't see your worth
* Value your roots and be proud of who you are
* Stay humble and grateful
* Learn from your mistakes and move forward without being too critical of yourself

Rosario Ozuna
July 23, 2024
Rio Grande City, TX

X

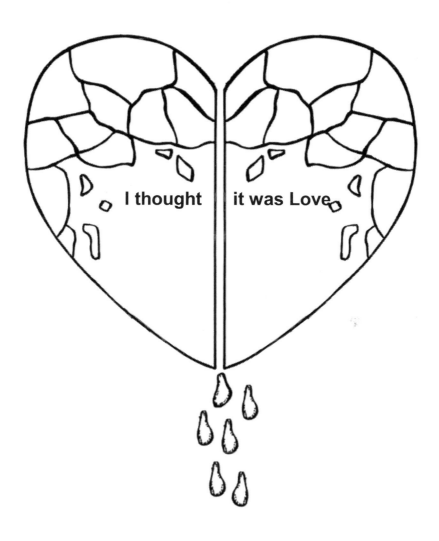

## I Control You, but I Love You

The minute I saw him
I knew he would be mine.
I didn't care that he had a girlfriend.
I knew I would do anything for him to notice me.
I planned my attack so he would leave her.

The minute I saw him
I knew he would be at my feet.
I bought a pre-paid cell phone and I started to text
messages to his girlfriend.
After a month of sending her text messages and
pretending to be someone else I convinced her I
would go out with him behind her back.
She finally broke up with him.

The minute I saw him
I knew his heart would eventually beat just for me.
I destroyed the pre-paid cell phone.
He begged her for a while for her to give him a
second chance as he did not know what girl she was
talking about.
She didn't believe him and finally he just gave up on
her too.

The minute I saw him
I knew how to manipulate him to be mine.
Two months after the breakup I pretended to bump
into him and he knocked my books out from my
hands.
His eyes crossed mine as we both kneeled down to
pick up my books.

3

The minute I saw him
I knew he would end up only loving me.
I gave him my number in a piece of paper as we both
picked up the books.
He smiled and he couldn't stop staring at me.

The minute I saw him
I knew we would end up together one way or the
other.
We began texting each other and after a month of
messaging each other he finally asked me out.
Our first date was a dream.
A message came in on his phone and I went insane
on him and I pulled his hair and punched him on his
shoulder.
He tried to calm me down and said, "Hold on, it's my
mom checking up on me!"
He started laughing at me.
"Oh honey, so sorry, I can't bear the thought of you
receiving a text from your ex." I exclaimed!
"No, I don't talk to her anymore, I only have eyes for
you." He calmly replied.

The minute I saw him
I knew he would have eyes only for me.
The next morning, I waited for him to be dropped off.
I greeted his mom. She told me she was so happy to
hear we were dating.
She waved her hand as she drove off.
I grabbed his hand and asked him, "I know we are
still getting to know each other, but I can't wait to be
your girlfriend — will you be my boyfriend?

He first stuttered and said it was too soon.
I gave him a kiss on his neck and whispered in his
ear, "But we are the perfect couple already, honey!"
He said, "Okay, I'm all yours!"
We both walked into the main hall of the school
holding hands.
He dropped me off by my first period classroom door.
He gave me a hug and a kiss on my cheek.
Everyone staring gave us happy smiles.

The minute I saw him
I knew he was my forever love.
I told him to meet me after each class and he did.
His friends were so pleased to see him happy again.
My friends were in disbelief when I told them how
quickly I had convinced him to be my boyfriend.
They all cheered me on and celebrated with me.
We were the talk of our entire school's topic and the
cutest couple, too!
I waited for him after first period class and he was
late.
I was so upset I slapped him because of the delay.
A friend of his was coming towards us, but he
pretended nothing had happened.
He reached out to me and kissed me on my cheek.
He then whispered in my ear, "I'm sorry, I will not be
late after your next class." I replied, "Okay baby!"

The minute I saw him
I knew he was just what I needed in my life.
He knew he was dating the most popular and
beautiful girl in school so I knew he was all mine.

He had football practice today and we had already made plans to go to the mall afterwards.

He didn't show up on time to pick me up.

Some of my college guy friends passed by the pick-up area and saw me standing there and they offered me a ride.

I left to the mall with my guy friends.

He shows up at the mall and sees me with my arms around one of my guy friend's neck.

He pushes the guy away and I pushed him against the railings super upset.

I told him, "You never arrived to pick me up, he is my friend and I came with him and the others, we are all just friends!" "It is you who I love!" "Right guys, all afternoon I've told you all how much I love him?" I replied.

The guys replied, "Oh yes, it is you who she loves bro, we are all just friends, we are like her brothers, dude!" "You see my love; they are like my brothers!" I exclaimed.

He then replied, "Okay. Let me take you home!"

I said, "No, go on yourself and my brothers will take me home."

He walked away with the saddest face and kept calling me all afternoon, yet I ignored his calls.

The minute I saw him
I knew he was my next target because I always get what I want.

He begged me and apologized for not picking me up to go to the mall.

I, of course accepted his apology after he begged me to forgive him.

The minute I saw him
I knew I would be his world.
It was Friday night and I attended his football game.
He was the best receiver our football team had.
I didn't like not one bit that the cheerleaders were
chanting his name.
He saw me get up from the stands and I left.
He looks at his coach and at his teammates, but he
still walks away from the football field to look for me.
He finds me. We were behind the football stadium
restrooms, and I was so upset that I pushed him
against the wall, causing him to fall, after which he
grabbed me by my knees.
I said, "You think I didn't see you while these
cheerleaders were chanting your name and you
smiled."
"Babe, I was playing a really good game that's why
they were chanting my name."
"Look, I even walked away from the game to look for
you."
"Please don't be mad," he replied.
I forgave him and I allowed him to go back to the
game.
His coach was upset, but he sent him back in the
game because he knew they would lose otherwise.

The minute I saw him
I knew his lips would only be mine.
On Monday, as we stopped by our locker, one of his
football buddies told him he shouldn't allow me to
treat him how I do.
I stepped in and told him, "You watch your words,
keep it up, and I'll have my dad fire yours!"

"Babe, back off; it's okay, I can handle this," he said.
"Oh yes you will, you're not allowed to be friends with this one anymore." "Tell him!" I told him.
He then replied, "Sorry Bro, I love her!"
"Get out of our way!" he continued to say.
"That's not love, dude!" his friend replied to him.
"Whatever man, you're just jealous because I'm dating the most popular and beautiful girl in school," he screamed at him.
We both walked away and he gave me a kiss and put his arm around my neck.

The minute I saw him
I knew he would be part of my life at any cost.
He received a text from his ex-girlfriend.
We were sitting by the benches behind the gym.
I pushed him off the bench and he hit himself on the arm and the back of his head as he bounced off.
I lost it and screamed at him.
I took away his phone and replied to her text, telling her to leave him alone... unless?
She stopped texting him.
I then told him that if he wanted me to trust him I needed the passwords to his phone and all of his social media apps.
He did not argue about it and smoothly gave me a kiss and told me, "I'll give them to you because I love you, babe!"
He got up and sat next to me on the bench.

The minute I saw him
I knew he would adore me and do as I pleased.
Suddenly, he told me that he was weary of the kind of person I am with him and that I overreact to
every situation.
He asked, "Let's talk about it, babe?"
I told him I had nothing to talk about and I also told him this, "Honey, there's plenty of others that wish they had me as their girlfriend, but I chose you."
"You're right, I'm sorry I even brought it up, babe!" he answered.
I then punched him in the stomach, and he dropped to his knees, gasping for air.
I told him, "That's for putting me through this."
He just stared at me.
I pretended like I was going to hit him with the back of my hand and he just curled up and covered his face with his hands.
I walked away and I left him there.
He was calling me and texting me all afternoon, but I gave him the silent treatment.

The minute I saw him
I knew I could walk all over him.
I forgave him the next day.
He invited me to go to his house.
We were enjoying the afternoon and suddenly one of his social media app notifications beeped.
I quickly took his phone away and he said, "It's just my friend, babe, he's tagging me on a post."
"Well, not anymore!" I told him and I blocked the friends I didn't like and oh boy I saw he still had his ex-girlfriend as a friend.

I posted a picture of us kissing, tagged her, and then blocked her from his social media app right after.
He just smiled and told me, "You're so crazy, Babe, but I love you like that!"
The minute I saw him
I knew he would fall crazy in love with me.
But I do not like to be called "crazy" although it's one of my terms.
So, I suddenly screamed at him, "How dare you call me crazy?" "I am not crazy!" "Wait babe, I didn't mean it like that!" he kept wailing.
"Wait, wait, wait!" he continued to scream.
"What are you doing?" he asked.
I turned red and I was so furious at him, I told him, "Here's your crazy!" "Don't forget, I control you, but I love you!"
I grabbed a butter knife he had by the night stand and I tried to stab him, so uncontrollably, not realizing the serious damage I had done to his eye.
He started to scream.
I dropped the knife and ran as his parents came into the room, screaming, "What's going on?"
I pushed them out of my way and ran out of the home.

The minute I saw her
I knew I should have walked away.
Because I knew she had the reputation of being out of it, jealous, possessive, and controlling.
But I just did not believe it.
I asked, "How can a beautiful and popular girl be so insecure?"

I was lucky, and the doctors were able to save my eye after five surgeries.
I wear glasses though and I attend therapy for my eye and for myself since this experience scarred me, but I know with time I'll be just fine.
My ex-girlfriend before this maniac one is now my friend.
We discovered it was my toxic ex-girlfriend that had caused us to break up.
As of now, I'm focusing on myself and I will never let anyone manipulate me into believing that their silly acts of jealousy and beatings are a reflection of their love for me.

The minute I saw her
I should have known better to just stay away, but her beauty captivated me and now I know why the most desirable girl in school didn't have a boyfriend then.

The minute I saw her
I shouldn't have helped her pick up her books.
She's presently serving a sentence in jail.
She sent me a letter and said, "The minute I saw you, I knew you were handsome, athletic, popular, but most importantly easy to control." "Don't forget, I control you, but I love you!" "I knew you would fall in my webs!" her lines continued to say.

Those three lines were more than enough to make me stop reading the letter.
I simply ignored those lines and the letter.
I crumbled it and threw it in the trash.
I never replied.

11

Piece by piece my heart understands that this nightmare has come to an end.

Her life is at halt, yet I can still go on!

## "But, He Must Really Love Me," I Said!

I am his girlfriend,
SO happy, I was!
A dream come true!
He loves me and I love him.
Perfect, we are, that's what I thought!
"But, HE must really love me," I said!
He proposed to prom with a beautiful bouquet of
balloons, the very next day!

He introduced me to his best friend,
SO happy, I was!
He called me a tramp!
We had our first fight, that's what I thought.
I wasn't even sure what had gone wrong!
All I did was shake his friend's hand, politely I thought.
He wouldn't answer my calls, he ignored my texts;
"But, HE must really love me," I said!
He showed up with a beautiful bouquet of balloons the
very next day!

I met his brother last night,
So happy, I was!
He accused me of hugging him too tight!
Sadly, we had our second fight!
I was so happy to meet his brother,
So, why does he doubt?
He pushed me against the locker,
And a teacher approached us.
He caressed my arm and asked, "Are you okay, Babe?"

I saw the teacher and before she could have asked me anything, I replied,
"Yes, I bumped into the locker door," "Silly me, I'm okay!"
The teacher walked away.
"But, HE must really love me," I said!
He showed up with a beautiful bouquet of balloons the very next day!

I met his parents,
SO happy, I was!
We sat down for dinner.
We had another fight, and oh my, he had that scary look in his eyes!
I dropped the water as I reached out for a piece of bread.
He pinched my leg under the table!
It hurt so much I had to excuse myself from the table and said, "I'll be right back, I need to use the ladies' room."
A few minutes after, he was waiting for me outside the restroom door.
He pushed me towards the door and grabbed me by my arms!
I told him, "Please stop, it hurts!" "You're hurting me, please STOP!"
His brother passed by, he quickly released me, gave me a hug and kissed me on the neck!
We returned to the table, but he was still holding me tight from the back of my neck.
We finished our dinner and I pretended I was okay.
His mom asked me, "Are you okay, my dear?"

As I rubbed the back of my neck and my arm, I replied,
"Silly me, I'm okay, I hit myself with the restroom door!"
The night ended and he took me home.
We sealed the night with a kiss and a tight hug!
"But, HE must really love me," I said!
He showed up with a beautiful bouquet of balloons the
very next day!

My friends are mesmerized with his charm,
And wish their boyfriends would give them a beautiful
bouquet of balloons every day. If they only knew, but I
know, "HE must really love me," I said!
He showed up with a beautiful bouquet of balloons the
very next day!

The day of the pep rally arrived,
SO happy, I was!
I was performing that day.
We had another argument, once again!
Behind the bleachers we were.
He didn't like the way the boys in the audience were
staring at me.
He pushed me against the brick wall,
I hit my lower back and bumped the back of my head!
I fell on my knees.
My friends passed by and saw me on the floor.
They rushed to help me!
They asked, "Are you okay?"
I softly replied, "Of course, silly me, I'm okay!" I tripped
with my gym bag and fell on my knees!"
"But, HE must really love me," I said!
He showed up with a beautiful bouquet of balloons
the very next day!

Three months into the relationship,
SO happy, I was!
Yet he never liked this or that about me!
He always found my flaws, so I thought the blame was
on me.
And, I continued to stay with him.
"But, HE must really love me," I said!
He always showed up with a beautiful bouquet of
balloons the very next day!

Excitedly, Prom Night, I await!
I went out with my friends to buy my prom gown.
I took too long with my friends buying the dress.
He was waiting for me at home.
My parents allowed him to do so.
I happily showed him the dress as I placed it on my
bed.
He was so upset, he grabbed me by my hair and
pushed me once again!
I hit the back of my head against the railing of my bed!
My prom dress beautifully lays on my bed, as I lay on
the floor covered in red.
He hugged my lifeless body on the floor and cowardly
ran away with blood on his hands!

While everyone wears their prom dresses, two days
after my death; I wear mine, too!

So happy, I AM NOT!!!!!
Because I never told anyone!
I would hide my bruises and always replied, "Silly me,
I'm okay!"

PIECE BY PIECE THE HEART UNDERSTANDS

I now lay in my coffin wearing my beautiful prom dress,
dancing into the light and whispering
good-bye!
"But, HE must really love me," I said!
He always showed up with a beautiful bouquet of
balloons the very next day!

From his cell, as if nothing had happened, he sends
them again and I received a beautiful bouquet of
balloons once more!
Those balloons were destroyed at my funeral,
AND so was I!
I no longer hurt, as I no longer exist.
I wish, I would have told someone, but silly me, always
pretended I was okay!
"But HE must really love me," I always said!
I was so WRONG!!!!!
Please don't be me, leave him as soon as you can!
So there will be NO MORE beautiful bouquets of
balloons the very next day!

Although it is too late for me, piece by piece my heart
understands! Does yours understand?

# She says it's Love

She says it's love
Yet, she screams at me for everything
She doesn't hear me out

She says it's love
Yet, she pretends I am not hurt
And always replies, "I was just joking!"

She says it's love
Yet, she blames me for everything
And claims it's my fault or says, "You made me do it!"

She says it's love
Yet, she's not empathetic
Just says, "You're overreacting!"

She says it's love
Yet, she manages to make my heart feel guilty
And claims, "I'm only doing this because I love you!"

She says it's love
Yet, the putdowns continue
My self-esteem is paying the price

She says it's love
Yet, the guilt trips don't come to a halt
And claims, "You just won't find someone better than me!"

She says it's love
Yet, she speaks ill of my friends
And I am isolated from them

She says it's love
Yet, I need to hide on her bad days
And claims, "You never give me my space!"

She says it's love
Yet, she asked for my phone and social media
passwords
And claims, "You're privacy is mine!"

She says it's love
Yet, piece by piece my heart finally understands
This is not love and I need this sick relationship to
end!

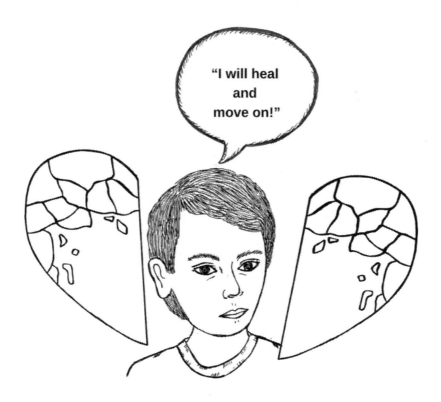

## He says it's Love

He says it's love
Yet, he screams at me for everything
He doesn't hear me out

He says it's love
Yet, he pretends I am not hurt
And always replies, "I was just joking!"

He says it's love
Yet, he blames me for everything
And claims it's my fault or says, "You made me do it!"

He says it's love
Yet, he's not empathetic
Just says, "You're overreacting!"

He says it's love
Yet, he manages to make my heart feel guilty
And claims, "I'm only doing this because I love you!"

He says it's love
Yet, the putdowns continue
My self-esteem is paying the price

He says it's love
Yet, the guilt trips don't come to a halt
And claims, "You just won't find someone better than me!"

He says it's love
Yet, he speaks ill of my friends
And I am isolated from them

He says it's love
Yet, I need to hide on his bad days
And claims, "You never give me my space!"

He says it's love
Yet, he asked for my phone and social media passwords
And claims, "You're privacy is mine!"

He says it's love
Yet, piece by piece my heart finally understands
This is not love and I need this sick relationship to end!

# He's so Lovely

He is so lovely
I love how he looks at me
As I walk down to my ELAR class

He is so lovely
I love how he bumps into me
While I wait for my lunch plate in the cafeteria line

He is so lovely
I love how he smiles
The minute our eyes cross each other by the gym

He is so lovely
I love how he touched my hand as we crossed each
other by the main hall and he gave me his cell phone
number on a piece of paper

He is so lovely
I love our text messages
Before we hugged our pillows at dusk and say, "I
wish you were here by my side!"

He is so lovely
I love that we have been texting each other for almost
five months
Everyone at school thinks of us as the "Perfect
Couple"

He is so lovely
I love we've gotten to know each other so much
And we've earned each other's trust

He is so lovely
My friends dared me to send him sensual pictures of me
And without hesitation I sent him five explicit selfies indeed

He is so lovely
He loved all of my selfies
He said I had a beautiful body

He is so lovely
He told me he loved me and texted "Good Night, my love!"
I believed him like a fool

He is not so lovely
I did not like the look on everyone's soul
As I walked into school the following day

He is not so lovely
So much for our trust
He poured that down the drain

He is not so lovely
I do not like that he shared my pictures with his friends
And they shared them with each of their other friends

He is not so lovely
My pictures were spread as quickly as a wild fire spreads
Even my friends were staring at me as if they had nothing to do with it

He is not so lovely
My so called friends don't want to be seen with me
So easily they forgot it was their dare

He is not so lovely
I don't like that the principal called me to his office
within an hour I had arrived to school
I walked into his office and the school cops and my
parents were waiting for me

He is not so lovely
I do not like this day at all
My parents were so disappointed and in disbelief

He is not so lovely
I just realized the severity of my infraction
I am only sixteen and the cops take me handcuffed

He is not so lovely
I don't like that those who I called "friends" turned
their backs on me
And the one who I trusted the most, betrayed me as
well

He is not so lovely
Was it love or the dare that betrayed me?
It doesn't matter as I should have known better

He is not so lovely
I was expelled from school
I am so frightened for what is to come

He is not so lovely
And I don't like that I am going in front of a judge
I realized I was wrong

He is not so lovely
I don't like that I was sentenced to two years'
probation
And I was charged with distribution of indecent
photographs of a minor

He is not so lovely
I don't like that he was just suspended from school
The evidence was just on my phone marked 'sent' to
his number
He is not so lovely
He was more clever than I was
He erased all of my images from everywhere on his
device and so did everyone else

He is not so lovely
I do not like what just happened to me
My life changed in a blink of an eye

He is not so lovely
I now understand I only hurt myself
But not only that, my reputation as the young lady
that I am has been tarnished

He is not so lovely
I learned my lesson, but a little too late
Now I am focused on trying to amend my mistake

He is not so lovely
I am taking it a day a time and complying with my
probation demands
I am not sure how this may impact my future

He is not so lovely
Please think of me when you try to send a sensual
selfie to someone you think you trust
Please don't let my story repeat!

Piece by piece my heart understands my daring
mistake and I will surely not repeat it again!

# The Thunderstorm

I felt the love since we met
But I still don't know you yet

I'm not loving all the words
Some of them strike my heart like a sword

The moment you began to see me different
Your soul became transparent

I don't like it
Not one bit

We need more time
Although you decline

I've always loved you
Indeed, you knew

Yet, you take advantage
And now my heart is wrapped in a bandage

Just like everything we've been through this pain is
real
But with time my heart will heal

Piece by piece my heart understands that just like a
severe thunderstorm disappears
This shall also pass and it'll be a bright sunny day
once again.

## She Doesn't Feel the Same

She doesn't feel the same
Even though her soul feels the pain
She doesn't miss you
And knows it's for the best

She doesn't feel the same
Even though her heart bleeds
She doesn't need you
Or your unfaithful heart

She doesn't feel the same
Even though her inner self is hurt
She understands she only deserves the very best
And knows this shall pass

She doesn't feel the same
Indeed, she reckons healing will take time
Yet, she knows that piece by piece her heart will
mend
And understands it was not meant to be and all will
soon be buried in the past!

## She was in Love

She was in love
Everyone could see it in her eyes
She loved him very much
But he could not see it

She was in love
She used to get lost in everything he uttered
She loved every part of him

She was in love
She misses his essence sometimes
He still appears in her dreams
But his foggy reality wakes her up each time

She was in love
She could feel it in her soul
She wishes she didn't remember him
But she's done with him

She was in love
But she knows it was never meant to be
She has moved on
This phase is in the past and her ailing heart has now
healed

She was in love
She finally realized it was the wrong heart
She knows her worth
And will never allow her heart to be mistreated ever
again

She was in love
Her heart is finally awake
It no longer bleeds for him
She finally found herself

She was in love with him
Not anymore, though
Indeed, she has a new love now
Piece by piece her heart understands that she is in
love with herself because self-love is her priority now
as it should have always been!

# She is Listening

Be careful what your lips whisper
She's listening
Although her ears are tired
Soon it will be too late

Be careful what your lips don't whisper
She's still listening
Although her ears don't hear you say much
Soon it will be too late

Be careful how you treat her
Her heart feels every move you make
She feels hurt
Soon it will be too late

Be careful if she stops loving you
She will know
She feels your indifference
Soon it will be too late

Be careful
You will regret it
Because one day
It will be too late for you to win her over
She will abandon your heart
And piece by piece her heart will understand leaving
to find herself is the ultimate best!

## Her Heart Beats Different

Her heart beats different
It changed
But only because it was ignored

Her heart beats different
It was too much
Her soul just had enough

Her heart beats different
It quit playing the waiting game
It missed feeling special

Her heart beats different
It was trapped in a web of lies
It stopped doubting itself

Her heart beats different
It felt unseen
It was slashed at the core

Her heart beats different
It felt unheard
It wanted to sing

Her heart beats different
It was not needy
But piece by piece the heart understands love was
just what it needed!

Love Exists

## I Love the Heart

I love the heart
    that has seen me in my bluest moments
I love the heart
    that has seen me in in my radiant moments
I love the heart
    that stays by my side no matter what
I love the heart
    that takes care of me every time I need it
I love the heart
    that holds me in his arms when I'm in pain
I love the heart
    that wipes the tears rolling down my cheeks
I love the heart
    whose soul laughs along mine
I love the heart
    that holds my hand
I love the heart
    that values me and treats me with respect
I love the heart
    that holds my heart dear to his
I love the heart
    that accepts mine as it is
I love the heart
    that contemplates my beauty as the wind
                      caresses my face
Piece by piece my heart understands that I will find
you because my heart will correspond your love!

## We Respect Each Other

I respect the love of my life and so does she
We do respect each other

I respect the love of my life and so does she
I do not hurt my lady's petals
Instead I caress her each time I am able

I respect the love of my life and so does she
I do not bully my better half
And neither does she

I respect the love of my life and so does she
I open the door to my car to the one that holds my
heart
While she smiles at me

I respect the love of my life and so does she
I take care of my better half by showing interest on
her
Not only on her sunny days, but also on the days
she's feeling blue

I respect the love of my life and so does she
I give my queen the throne she deserves and so
does she
I am her king

I respect the love of my life and so does she
I don't raise my voice at my lady
I calm down and allow her to express her feelings
and thoughts

I respect the love of my life and so does she
I listen to her conversations
And she listens to mine

I respect the love of my life and so does she
We've learned to empathize with each other
Even if sometimes our feelings disagree
We find our common ground

I respect the love of my life and so does she
We support each other's passions
We are there for each other
Every step of the way

I respect the love of my life and so does she
We trust each other
We give each other our own space
Each time one of us needs it

I respect the love of my life and so does she
I don't control her
She has her friends and I have mine
We respect that about each other

I respect the love of my life and so does she
I am observant of her different looks and praise her
each time
She commends me, too

I respect the love of my life and so does she
Even when something bothers us both, we are
honest with each other
We find a way to discuss it

I respect the love of my life and so does she
We don't make assumptions
We always ask each other for clarification
If we don't understand

I respect the love of my life and so does she
I take her out
We visit places she likes
Other times, the places I prefer

I respect the love of my life and so does she
We try our best to balance our relationship
We always let each other know our plans
So we can arrange our outings accordingly

I respect the love of my life and so does she
We are not perfect, but we treat each other with the
full power of "respect"
We try our best to be better each and every day

I respect the love of my life and so does she
We both respect each other's boundaries
Piece by piece our hearts understand
Respect is the way for a relationship to flourish and
become stronger every day!

## The Promise

My heart is full
You are the secret spice
And the sweet taste to my daily life
You are the one behind my dreams
Always supporting my heart's desires
Even when my soul doubts
Your lips have the perfect words
Which inspire my motor to keep on going
All that your soul whispers becomes a reality
Although sometimes the day's circumstances shatter
my heart
I end up with an abundance of bottled feelings
But your ear is kind
Always ready and attentive
Other times my heart is overjoyed
And once again your arms take me in with pride
No matter what the world throws at me
You've always been there
Keeping the promise you once whispered,
"I promise I'll always be there for you, no matter
what!"
Piece by piece your heart continues to understand
and keeps your wholesome PROMISE!

## My Friend is My Soulmate

Magical my life has been because of you
You've always been there for me

"Fabulous life" is an understatement
Radiant and positive you've always remained
Inspiring me every step of the way
Endearing your heart has always been
Nourishing my soul with beautiful expressions of love
is your favorite pastime
Daringly we surpass each other's expectations

Identical souls we possess
Sacred is our friendship

Motivating me to follow my dreams is your motto
You are my best friend and confidant

Safe, I feel with you
Overjoyed and
Unbeatable I feel when you are with me
Love unifies us
Majestic is our relationship
Attentive and
Thoughtful you've always been, therefore
Everlasting our friendship and love will be

Piece by piece you win my heart and it understands
that not only you are my friend, but my soulmate. We
are deeply in love with one another!

## We Don't Give Up

We don't give up on each other
This feeling changes everything
This is what I love about us
We believe in one another

We don't give up on each other
Instead, we care for one another
We always find a way to make it through our shady moments
We know half of the battle is already won

We don't give up on each other
Instead, we value each other
We always listen to one another
We know our hearts are one

We don't give up on each other
Instead, we prioritize one another
We are always each other's number one
We trust each other

We don't give up on each other
Instead, we know each other very well
We always give each other space
We respect each other

We don't give up on each other
Instead we are there for one another
Piece by piece our hearts understand that all of these
only makes our love stronger!

# My Heart WILL NOT let YOU Go

My heart is here
      thinking of you
          wishing you were with me
My heart is here
      willing to give up anything
          just to see your stunning face
My heart is here
      feeling lonely
          without your hugs
My heart is here
      knowing I will never hear
          your voice
My heart is here
      waking up
          feeling empty everyday
My heart is here
      screaming and searching for you
          in the bright blue skies
My heart is here
      crying because it misses
          you wholeheartedly
My heart is here
      waiting until our hearts
          meet once again
My heart is here
      broken in pieces but understands that
          until that day comes
             my heart will not
               let you go!

# Love WILL find Me

I close my eyes
Pondering if love exists
I feel my heart beat like a drum as I tap my chest
It's like listening to the beat of an ill-favored song

I close my eyes
Wondering if love does exist
I still hear my heart pounding loudly in my ears as I
also tap my foot following its rhythm
Only to remind me that I've been hurt too many times

I close my eyes
Again doubting that love exists
This pondering repeats just like an unpleasant
scenario in my head
Yet, I still try to grasp where my heart may have gone
wrong

I close my eyes
Wondering when will I find my soulmate
Suddenly my thoughts whisper,
"You just wait, your match is soon to come!"

I close my eyes
I realize love does exist
The painful experiences make me doubt
But I don't lose hope
I still believe

I know my heart understands that piece by piece
love will find me soon!

63

# Watering the Fire

My eyes see you
Your eyes see me
Yet we argue
Nevertheless we can't be separate
Our souls cry in despair
Every time they're on fire
Due to the ongoing pain
Perhaps it's not right
But these disagreements help us get better
acquainted
These are a must
Once the fire is watered
Piece by piece our eyes reunite
And our hearts understand each other
Calmly we discuss our differences
And fall in love all over again!

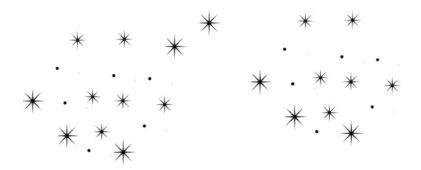

## It Takes an Inner Force to Believe in Oneself

Continue
believing
in
YOURSELF!

## The Mirror

My eyes see it in the mirror
I am beautiful
Indeed, I am

My eyes see it in the mirror
I am beautiful
My lips tell me everyday

My eyes see it in the mirror
I am beautiful
My heart whispers it to my ear

My eyes see it in the mirror
I am beautiful
Inside and out

My eyes see it in the mirror
I am beautiful
My character traits work in harmony

My eyes see it in the mirror
I am beautiful
My heart is genuine and doesn't speak deliberately

My eyes see it in the mirror
I am beautiful
My inner self is confident

My eyes see it in the mirror
I am beautiful
My soul is kind to others

My eyes see it in the mirror
I am beautiful
Polite is my favorite word

My eyes see it in the mirror
I am beautiful
My heart is passionate about life regardless

My eyes see it in the mirror
I am beautiful
My hands are always at service

My eyes see it in the mirror
I am beautiful
I don't bully not even my reflection

My eyes see it in the mirror
I am beautiful
I am not a bystander

My eyes see it in the mirror
I am beautiful
All my deeds are saved in my heart

My eyes see it in the mirror
I am beautiful
I value others and myself

Do you see it in the mirror?
Yes! You are beautiful
Piece by piece the heart understands
It gives, forgives, and lives for others!

## Insecurity

She misses her voice
But she knows she has one
She doesn't know how to scream at the world

She misses her voice
There's been moments when she's had the courage
to say what's in her mind
Yet, her second voice stops her

She misses her voice
She's frightened to be a disappointment
She doubts herself almost always

She misses her voice
She lives with this monster on a daily basis
Each time she builds the courage to show the world a
piece of her, she loses control

She misses her voice
This animal pulls her down again
Yet, she searches inside and finds the courage to
move on

She misses her voice
She takes a huge breath and closes her eyes
She visualizes herself on top of a mountain and
screams her lungs out while stepping on the beast's
head

She misses her voice
And the monster growls, "You can't do it!"
But, she continues to crush his horrific head

She misses her voice
But her heart speaks to her and claims, "You've got
this!"
She kicks him off the mountain and it vanishes into
thin air

She recuperates her voice
She breathes clean air and speaks her mind as she
believes in herself; the monster has faded away
Ultimately, piece by piece her heart understands that
she has a lot to share with the world and that her
voice matters too!"

"You've got this!"

# A Little Voice Speaks to Me

Drizzling from the sky
I look up although I am shy

The raindrops roll down my cheeks
My arms also extend and take a peek

With my head tilted back my body spins
No, the raindrops do not feel like pins

Instead they softly caress my skin
Thinking and reflecting during this time I've always
been

I stop swirling while staring at the clouds
As I no longer have any doubts

A little voice speaks to me
"You see, you are free!"

"Don't worry, just go on!"
It's almost dawn

I take a last deep breath
The smell of the crisp rain reminds me of my strength

That's the reason I love dancing in the rain
And I will continue to do it over and over again

Rainy days like this, I enjoy
My heart is full of joy

Don't forget to enjoy life, especially on those rainy days
It is these days that piece by piece our heart understands we are resilient and strong and we can overcome any obstacles we might face!

# Courageous Wings

With courageous wings she soars
Her soul is determined
Fearlessly she glides into her dreams
And conquers

With courageous wings she soars
She's endured everything with great fortitude
Her tenacity has never abandoned her
She's firm in her beliefs

With courageous wings she soars
Her heart is daring
Valiantly she floats above all
Regardless of what other lips mumble

With courageous wings she soars
Her persistence to continue to savor her acts is
sacrificial
Boldly she drifts from the unsuitable
She knows her worth and her capabilities

With courageous wings she soars
Her essence does not betray her
Her secret self is always by her side
Cheering her on

With courageous wings she soars
Always whispering in her ear
"Continue to be tenacious, believe, and don't forget to
pursue relentlessly!"
Piece by piece her heart understands that her wings
will always spread freely and reach the sky!

79

## Their Opinion

Some have an opinion of you
But their beliefs are based on their reality
Not yours

Some have an opinion of you
But, you'll always be who you are no matter what
You will not betray your soul by deceiving your
integrity based on what their lips whisper

Some have an opinion of you
But their opinion has no meaning in your world
You solely believe in yourself

Some have an opinion of you
You know what you inspire
Your heart knows where you're going in life

Some have an opinion of you
But your soul has endured so much
You know where you stand

Some have an opinion of you
Regardless, you will not betray yourself
Because you know who you truly are

Some have an opinion of you
But you ignore it
Indeed, piece by piece your heart understands that
you're worth more than just a vague opinion!

## As Long as I Don't Give Up

Here I am believing and knowing I can do it
No matter what obstacles get in the way
I don't give up
I always find a way to move forward

A mountain obstructed my way
I couldn't move it
I didn't give up
I went around it

It took longer than what I expected
The ride was rough
I didn't give up
I walked the long path until the end

Although I found a way to continue
There were still many other boulders in the way
I climbed each one
Until I saw the light

No matter what gets in the way
I will go around it, over it, or under it
I don't give up
I'll face it, destroy it, and deal with it

I face life as it comes
Because my heart understands that piece by piece I
can accomplish anything
As long as I don't give up
And continue to believe in myself!

## Don't Forget

Don't forget
You didn't get this far just because
No matter what you're going through
There is light at the end of the tunnel
Things always happen for a reason
Even though the heart doesn't know the reasons
Don't forget
You just keep going
If you fall then get up
Don't yield to believe
Piece by piece your heart will understand and will not
give up!

## Today

Today is a new day
Today gives you a second opportunity to do what you
wish for
Today is affording you more time to try again
Today is another day to believe in what you do
Today is the day
The day that you get up again and just try one more
time
Piece by piece each day provides a different
opportunity for your heart to understand that you can
do it. You just have to keep trying and don't yield to
believe in yourself!

## Shine

Shine and illuminate your life as bright as it can be
Hard work it will take, but you will beam
Imagine yourself glowing while pursuing your goal
and you will attain success
Never give up and find that inner strength and you
will glow
Endless are the opportunities life will provide you to
shine when you believe in yourself

Piece by piece and one day at a time your heart will
shine and understand that trusting yourself will help
you reach those shiny stars!

Shine, glow, and illuminate your path with positive
thoughts and you'll succeed!

## Glow

*G*low is already in your heart
*L*ight up your path by believing in yourself
*O*btainable your goals will always be, but you must trust in yourself
*W*ork hard, believe, and don't give up and your brightness will always prevail!

Piece by piece your heart puts your goals together and understands that glowing is your priority!

Who Wears the True Crown?

# Feeling the Pain

She secretly walks feeling the pain
Deep down she hurts
Her bestie turned her group of friends against her
They speak horrors of her
Yet, it's all lies
But she still manages to smile

She secretly walks feeling the pain
Little does anyone know
All because of a boy
They were just friends
But the bestie secretly liked the boy and she didn't
know
Despite the lies, she still manages to speak to them

She secretly walks feeling the pain
She keeps everything bottled up
Her ears hear more lies about her
The boy defends her and explains to the bestie
He only asked her for math help
Defiantly she still walks the halls with pride

She secretly walks feeling the pain
Without a true friend to listen to her
She still shows up and hangs out with the group
Her bestie ignores her without whispering a word
The boy apologizes to her and knows her group of
friends are wrong
Regardless of the situation and so many speaking ill
of her she hides the pain with a smile in her eyes

She secretly walks feeling the pain
Wishing she could no longer hurt
Finally her bestie speaks to her
She gives her version of the story
The bestie hugs her and whispers, "We are all good!"
Her kind heart believes her words

She secretly walks feeling the pain
Expecting the group to accept her again
They all make plans to go to the school dance
The boy asks her to the dance and confesses he
does like her
She refuses the invite
She explains she only wants to be friends

She secretly walks feeling the pain
Thinking it repeats again
But this time the boy does like her
Rumor spreads like a wildfire
The group of friends ignore her once again
Her heart continues to ache

She secretly walks feeling the pain
The bestie is very popular and convinces the boys
not to ask her to the dance
Unfortunately, everyone is scared of her
Because of her despiteful prior acts
Everyone goes along with the bestie and they believe
her lies
When she hears that no one will ask her to the
dance, she doesn't know what to do but cry in
despair

She secretly walks feeling the pain
But what these don't know is that she has a
childhood friend at a neighboring school
Rumor spreads once again
The bestie plans a despiteful plan with the group of
friends
All of them make a pact
Indeed, she's hurt and doesn't know about the
scheme, but still manages to give them the benefit of
the doubt

She secretly walks feeling the pain
The boy asks the bestie to go to the dance with him
She's always loved the boy
She's entitled because she thinks she got what she
wanted
Dance night arrives
She chooses to forget about the pain and tries to
enjoy the night

She secretly walks feeling the pain
She arrives to the dance with her handsome
childhood friend
She looks stunning in her long slim beautiful red
gown with a gorgeous shimmery train following the
dress
As she walks in everyone turns to look at her
including the boy
The bestie does not like it and makes a growling face
She still ignores and approaches the table with all the
friends and their dates

She secretly walks feeling the pain
They try to sit down in two empty chairs by the table
The bestie tells them they can't sit there
Because their purses are there
She starts looking around for another table
Her childhood friend tells her not to worry as they will
be dancing all night and they don't need a place to sit

She secretly walks feeling the pain
She is definitely having fun and enjoying herself with
her childhood handsome friend
She spots a friend she has in her homeroom class
They stop by and say hello
She offers them two chairs
They joined her and talk the night away

She secretly walks feeling the pain
Little did she know what was coming up next
Ballots start going around
Everyone votes for the dance king and queen
The principal prepares to announce the winners
The bestie gets ready to get up
"SURPRISE!" The bestie did not get the crown and
her jaw drops when she hears the new queen

She secretly walks feeling the pain
The boy wins king and she wins queen
She is in shock and radiantly smiles in disbelief
Her childhood friend tells her to go on and claim her
crown
Everyone applauds and screams her name except for
the table where the bestie and the group of friends sit

She secretly walks feeling the pain
Everyone has reached their limits and they've had it
with the bestie and her group of friends
What these girls didn't know is that a bystander heard
their malevolent plan
The bystander couldn't hear everything to the "T"
But he did capture that they were to embarrass her
somehow on the dance floor
He quickly spreads the evil plan and the rest of the
student body finally figures out that she was their
victim and everything that was murmured about her
were strictly lies

She secretly walks feeling the pain
They decided to surprise her by voting for her as
queen for the night
The king and queen danced their first dance
Then the principal announces for everyone to join the
king and queen on the dance floor
The bestie approaches the dance floor and cuts in
between them
To everyone's surprise she carries her evil plan
She steps on the train of her beautiful gown
Her childhood friend sees what's going on and runs
to the center of the dance floor
Everyone else stops dancing and are in disbelief of
what they just witnessed

She secretly walks feeling the pain
The bestie laughs as the boy pushes her off the
dress
"Oops!" She exclaims
He yells at her, "What is wrong with you?"
And walks away to check on his queen
Everyone else looks at the bestie disappointedly
She screams, "Why are you all staring?"
"It's just a dress!"
The dress splits open from the back of her waist

She secretly walks feeling the pain
Her childhood friend takes off his red tie and places it
around her waist
Her childhood friend hugs her, cleans the tears rolling
down her rosy cheeks and floats away with her on
the dancing floor
Her gown looks even more beautiful with that red
bow hanging on the back of her waist
As it was the ultimate touch to the dress
The bestie's eyes lit up in flames once again
The boy tells her, "Enough is enough, just leave her
alone!"

She secretly walks feeling the pain
The principal and a chaperone grab the bestie from
the arm
As they witnessed what she did
The principal calls her parents
They have her exit the dance
And is expelled for the remainder of the school year
As there is zero tolerance for bullying

She secretly walks feeling the pain
A night that should have been destroyed
Ended up been one her best
She enjoyed the rest of the dance with good company
She made a new group of friends at the table with her friend from her homeroom class
She just looked at the bestie and nodded her head as she was taken away
The rest of the group of friends couldn't even see her as they felt ashamed

She now walks freely and does not feel the pain
She has new friends in her life
In the days to come, the boy continued to ignore the ex-bestie's texts and phone calls
He joined her group of friends and apologized to her
He also explained that he had nothing to do with the ex-bestie's evil plan
He extended his hand and asked her if they could be friends and she happily shook his hand

She now walks freely and does not feel the pain
She made changes in her life
Her loving heart couldn't see her group of friends for their evil intentions, but the mask finally fell off
Although it took piece by piece her heart finally understands that not all of her so called "friends" are true
The ones she least expected turned out to be better friends than the group of friends she previously had
Everyone that thought ill of her apologized and finally saw her noble heart!

## FRIENDS

Friends fix each other's crowns
Reachable, they always are and
Illumination for each other's path in needy times
they supply
Endless advice they provide
Nurturing souls they possess
Dedicated to the friendship they've always been
Supportive, sincere, and they always stand by you
no matter what!

Piece by piece your heart understands your friends' intentions and it recognizes those that wear the true crown!

# MY FRIEND

**My** FRIEND is …

*F*abulous, you've always been and always will be
*R*adiating so much sunshine in my life
*I*nspiring everyone as always with your
*E*ndearing attitude and always
*N*ourishing my soul with your wise advice
*D*aring as always we beat the odds together

And piece by piece my heart understands you're my
true friend because you are selfless, therefore our
friendship stands strong and continues to shine!

## You and Her

You and her had a beautiful relationship
But you let them change your mind about her

You and her had a beautiful relationship
But you allowed their nonsense to tell you otherwise

You and her had a beautiful relationship
But their thoughts about her had more weight than
the manner you knew her heart

You and her had a beautiful relationship
But they couldn't bear the thought that you both
simply had a pure and sincere friendship

You and her had a beautiful relationship
But she was hurt because of the way you treated her
suddenly

You and her had a beautiful relationship
Yet, you refused to change and continued listening to
their ill gossip regarding her

You and her had a beautiful relationship
Yet, your indifference continued

You and her had a beautiful relationship
But, she put a stop to it and the relationship vanished

You and her had a beautiful relationship
She realized everything happens for a reason

You and her had a beautiful relationship
She understands a friendship cannot be forced

You and her had a beautiful relationship
But she knows her worth

You and her had a beautiful relationship
Although she's hurt, she is still kindhearted

You and her had a beautiful relationship
Her heart has forgiven you and those who badly
spoke about her

You and her had a beautiful relationship
She knew she's not perfect, but neither were you or
any of them

You and her had a beautiful relationship
But, piece by piece her heart understands that this
friendship was not meant to be!

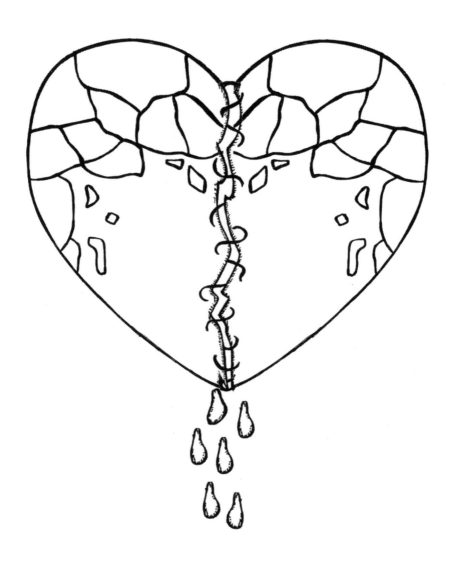

# Don't let them hurt Alone

When you care about someone
You don't let them hurt alone
They may imply they're okay
But they are in dismay

When you care about someone
You don't let them hurt alone
Don't forget to check on them
These situations make them feel condemned

When you care about someone
You don't let them hurt alone
These circumstances make them feel scare
But, a text message, a phone call or a voice message
shows that you care

When you care about someone
You don't let them hurt alone
They perhaps won't reply right away
But these messages help make their day

When you care about someone
You don't let them hurt alone
Keep reaching out because you are making a
difference
Knowing that your presence is their reassurance

When you care about someone
You don't let them hurt alone
Your friendship does matter
Knowing you're visible will help them feel better

When you care about someone
You don't let them hurt alone
Yes, they need their space
But with your support they'll heal at their own pace

When you care about someone
You don't let them hurt alone
Just don't give up and be patient
Because the final outcome will be pleasant

When you care about someone
You don't let them hurt alone
Piece by piece your heart understands their situation
And their heart understands the proper time to finally
cure!

## Hurtful Heart

My heart is hurt
So is yours
There is no way two hearts in pain can continue
The day has come to let each other go
But I still ask, can two broken hearts remain as
friends?

Your heart is hurt
So is mine
There's no way these two hearts can stay together
The day has come to end this
But I still ask, can two broken hearts remain as
friends?

My heart bleeds
So does yours
There's no way these two hearts can be mended
The day we never anticipated has shown its radiant
face
But I still ask, can two broken hearts remain as
friends?

Once my heart heals
Once your heart heals
Perhaps both hearts can reunite
But until that day wakes up
My heart understands it needs healing time piece by
piece
Therefore, it whispers "Being friends is not yet
possible!"

Life Molds the Heart

## Life is Like a Flower

Life is like a flower
Beautiful and kind
It all depends on your heart's perspective

Life is like a flower's petal
Smooth but breakable at times
But your heart decides

Life is like a flower's roots
Gentle but fragile
It is admissible to cry

Life is like a flower's pot soil
Dark and hard sometimes
But sprinkle some water and the soil will revive

Life is like a flower's scent
Fresh and crisp
Just like your heart when it renews after breaking

Life is like a flower's thorns
Some have them and others don't
They're prickly but are used as a shield that
protects them from harm

Life is like a flower's stem
Crooked or straight sometimes
But your heart decides which way to follow

Life is the beauty of a flower
It may break at the stem
Its petals may fall
It may be thirsty for water
It may lack sunshine
It may have sharp thorns
But its roots are not damaged so it will try once again
to revive
Just like our life continues piece by piece after so
many ups and downs!

## Tears and Smiles

Tears and smiles
Are important
Each depicts a story in my life

Tears and smiles
Help me decide
I choose me

Tears and smiles
Taught me a lesson
I choose self-love

Tears and smiles
Have advised me well
I choose self-care

Tears and smiles
Have shaped who I am
I am stronger than ever

I choose tears
Slowly piece by piece my heart understands
Without tears of pain or joy I wouldn't be here now

I choose smiles
Slowly piece by piece my heart understands
Without my daily grins I wouldn't appreciate my blue
moments

My heart decides to embrace both!

# The Accent

I love my accent
It depicts my story
It reflects the battles I've endured to learn the
language
It has witnessed too much as I've learn to read and
speak the language

I love my accent
It has so much to say, if you pay attention
It knows whom I've spoken to
I always listen so I'll learn more

I love my accent
It understands the challenges I've faced to pronounce
each word and each phrase in each conversation I've
had
It's always been by my side

I love my accent
It is who I am
Although I've learn a new language
My accent still reflects me

I love my accent
Soft, low, deep, or high it's still all about me
And those around me understand
This accent will always be heard

I love my accent
Accent or not, I'm proud because I can speak the
lovely English language
My accent depicts my dear heritage
And the new part of my life

Piece by piece my heart understands the importance
of my accent. I take pride in it as it is a huge part of
my heart. My accent is both of my worlds combined!

Humble

Grateful

## Humble

Ego only creates webs in your soul
Making you think you're on top of the world
While smashing other's brightness
Is not acceptable
When in time we all share the same opportunities

Your inner soul must submit
Feel deserving, yet grateful
To those who helped you ascend
Burn the arrogant ego
Acknowledge those on your path to success

Indeed, embrace it all
But never overweigh your mind with feelings of
greatness
Their eyes will see you for who you truly are
Once you recognize this
Your wisdom and acceptance will make you kneel
and vow

Only then that ego will dissipate
Indeed, you'll realize it was wrong
By accepting you'll wake up from your royal dream
Your heart finally pumps up piece by piece in
excitement
And understands that staying humble is the way!

Humble          Grateful

## The Mistake

My heart aches
It is still in disappointment
I knew better
Yes it's difficult to understand
But I will find a way to march on

My heart aches
It is still in disbelief
For what it's seen
But, I have it in me to believe again
I will flourish as I always do

My heart aches
It cries and holds that mistake tight
But I must prove to it that I've learned
Only then I can accept myself
And move on

My heart smiles
I've seen the light
I understand life has its ups and downs
Although I can't control the future
I can free my mistake

My heart smiles
This mistake does not define me
Indeed, I will not torment myself anymore
It is piece by piece that my heart understands to learn
from it and continue my path
I no longer hurt as it is part of the past!

# Piece by Piece the Heart Understands

Piece by piece
A heart bleeds on a daily basis
It does not receive what it needs
Disappointed, but it attempts one more time

Piece by piece
A heart continues to break
It does not know how much more it will take
Although it's weary, it endures

Piece by piece
A heart is in distress
But it refuses to be depressed
Indeed, it pumps itself to push forward

Piece by piece
A heart cries
Please tell the world to stop whispering lies
Because the earmuffs have finally fallen off

Piece by piece
A heart screams
"Enough, you're not part of my goals and dreams!"
Its limits have been reached

Piece by piece
A heart regains its value and self-control
It is done playing the victim's role
It took a series of setbacks and heartaches
But it finally understands

Piece by piece only makes the heart stronger
Piece by piece it slowly puts itself together
Piece by piece it believes in itself
Piece by piece it begins to live again
Piece by piece it conquers all of its fears and the
unknown
Piece by piece the heart understands life is prickly
but also that persistence is the key to move on!

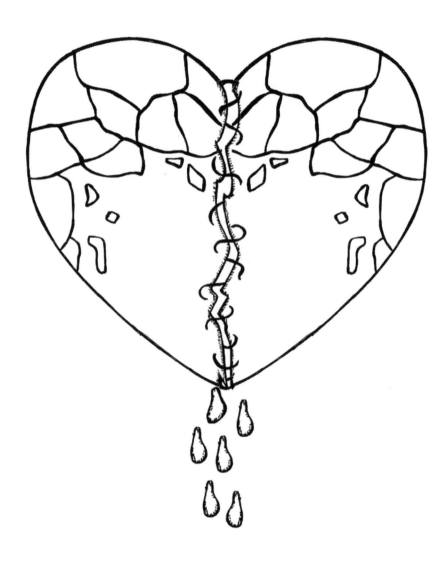

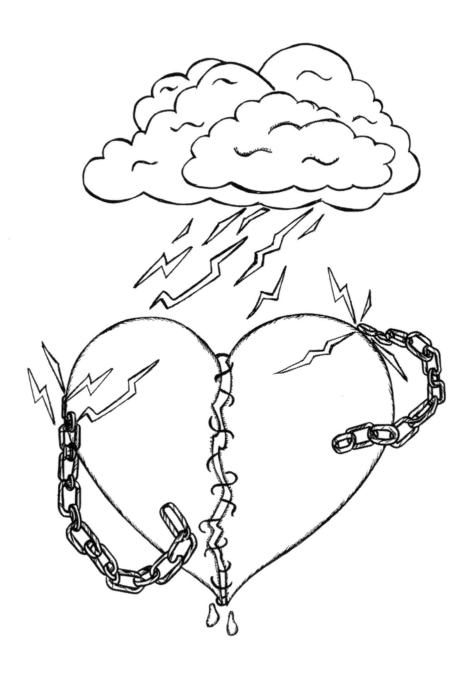

# Hurtful Past

Don't let the hurtful past keep you from enjoying what the present has to offer

Don't let the hurtful past mold you into the ill version you see on others

Don't let the hurtful past dictate your future

Don't let the hurtful past chain you up

Don't let the hurtful past define your heart

Don't let the hurtful past speak a distorted version of yourself

Although you can't change your hurtful past, you can accept it as it is part of you, but step over it before it steps all over you

Although you can't change your hurtful past, you can mold your heart to forgive and see yourself as the beautiful and understandable person that you truly are

Piece by piece your heart understands and it will break the chains this hurtful past has on your soul only to realize that it will strengthen you instead!

Accept,
Forgive and Move On

## The Plea

My mouth was rude
Spitting selfish words
My eyes witnessed your suffering
You bleed because of my evil words
I wish I could whisper them back
And tangle them up in my tongue
Or swallow them down my throat
But how?
How else can I repair your shattered soul?
Please ask your heart to forgive mine
Indeed, no excuses
Piece by piece my heart understands it is at fault
"I am sorry!"
"I am so sorry!"
"So sorry!"
"I am deeply SORRY!"

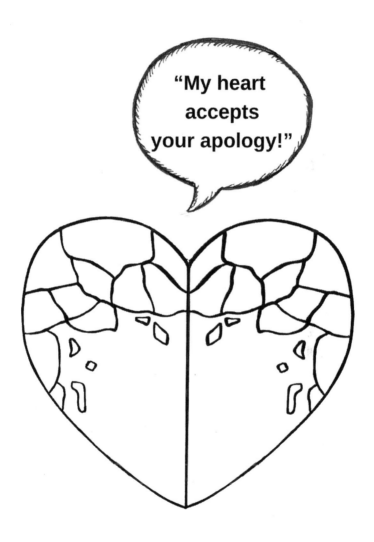

# Acknowledgments

First and foremost, I want to express my gratitude to the Lord for blessing me with a beautiful life and the ongoing opportunity to be here. Thank you for helping me realize my dreams; I feel truly blessed and trust my life in Your hands.

I also extend heartfelt thanks to my dear husband and beloved sons for their unwavering support. Your belief in me and encouragement to pursue my dreams mean everything. This book would not have come to fruition without your steadfast backing, especially following my first.

I am eternally thankful to my dear friend and author, Miracle Austin (known for the *Doll* trilogy, *Boundless*, and *Fright Bites*), for her invaluable guidance, encouragement, and unwavering support in everything I pursue. Your friendship means the world to me, and I deeply appreciate your time in reading my book, as well as your thoughtful feedback and review.

I want to express my gratitude to my friend and colleague, Nancy Yvette Peña, who is a Middle School Counselor, for taking the time to read my book and share your thoughts. Your feedback and review were incredibly valuable to me, and I truly appreciate your support.

I am grateful to all the authors I've encountered throughout my career, whose beautiful writings continue to motivate and inspire me.

I want to extend my gratitude to my editor, Aldo Gonzalez, who has worked closely with me to breathe new life into *Piece by Piece the Heart Understands*, our second book together.

I also want to thank Mia Anahi Martinez for her diligent work in bringing my vision to life with the beautiful book cover. Your talent is exceptional, and I wish you continued success in all your endeavors.

To all the readers, I deeply appreciate you taking the time to read the synopsis of my book, feeling intrigued, selecting it, and dedicating time to read it. My hope is that you find enjoyment in its pages and always remember, "You're your number one!" Prioritize your safety and reach out for assistance when needed. Keep moving forward and pursue your 'GLOW'—never let the light within you fade!

To my parents, brothers and sisters, my deepest gratitude for their ongoing love and support in all that I do. But, a very special thank you to my mom for raising a resilient and tough girl with a heart, despite the circumstances!

Finally, to my beautiful first grandchild, Emily Ayme Ozuna, and to my future grandchildren whom I haven't yet met: I already love each of you very much. My wish is for you to one day read my books and understand that the key to reaching your goals is to never stop believing in yourself, no matter what! Respect yourselves and others. Always think before you act, and follow your 'GLOW' at all times!

# About the Author

Rosario Ozuna is a published author with a deep passion for reading and writing. She is a poet, and an advocate for literacy. She enjoys writing poems and reflections about everyday experiences and what inspires her. She is a graduate of Sam Houston State University at Huntsville, Texas with a Master's Degree in Library Science.

She is a middle school librarian in South Texas. When she's not promoting her library, or writing, she enjoys creating book trailers for her YouTube channel, One Book or Novel at a Time. She also enjoys drawing on her spare time.

She was born in Mexico, but was raised in the Rio Grande Valley in South Texas. She lives with her family in Texas. *The Tears Behind the Smile: Poems and Reflections from the Heart* was her debut poetry book in 2023. *Piece by Piece the Heart Understands* is her second poetry book.

Made in the USA
Columbia, SC
12 January 2025

b0d1ce58-4255-49e6-8ff9-6b9b3cc8fee6R01